Coat of a Thousand Lives: Threads of the Forgotten

The Third in the Series of

Seven Books

The Origin of The Loveday Method®

A Heptalogy

By

Geoffrey Loveday

The Origin of The Loveday Method: Coat of a Thousand Lives

Author: Geoffrey Loveday Copyright © 2025 by Geoffrey Loveday - All Rights Reserved.

The right of Geoffrey Loveday to be identified as author of this work has been asserted by the author in accordance with section 77 and 78 of the Copyright, Designs and Patents Act 1988.

First Published in 2025
ISBN 978-1-917978-06-4 (Paperback)
ISBN 978-1-917978-07-1 (Hardback)
ISBN 978-1-917978-08-8 (E-Book)
Book cover design and layout by: Geoffrey Loveday

Published by:
Mindlayers Publishing
35-37 Ludgate Hill,
London England,
EC4M 7JN
www.liverpoolhypnosis.co.uk

Authors and publishers cannot be held responsible for any consequences that result from the usage of information in this book. The author or the publisher assumes no responsibility or liability for how you use the information contained herein.

A CIP catalogue record for this title is available from the British Library.

All rights reserved. No part of this book may be reproduced or translated by any form or by any means, electronic or mechanical, including photocopying, recording or by any information storage and retrieval system without written permission from the author.

The novel is entirely a work of fiction. The names, characters, and incidents portrayed in it are the work of the author's imagination. Any resemblance to actual persons, living or dead, events or localities is entirely incidental. The views expressed by the fictional characters do not necessarily reflect the views of the author.

I wonder where life will take us now …

And so the journey begins.

Let me take you on this magical adventure.

Contents

THE HEART BEHIND THE WORDS.................................. 7
    About the Author:..7
    Dedication:..9
    Inspiration:..12
    Why I write this:..13

"The Soul Remembers", by Geoffrey Loveday *16*

What are the Threads of the Forgotten? *20*
    This is a story that must be told 25

Coat of a Thousand Lives... *29*
    The Beginning: The Return of the Hidden Ones 31

Chapter One: "The Scribe's Silence"............................... *35*
Chapter Two: "The Midwife's Fire" *40*
Chapter Three: "The Last Flight".................................... *45*
Chapter Four: "The Warning"... *51*
Chapter Five: "The Temple of the Silent Star" *57*
Chapter Six: Sarah - The First Thread *62*
Chapter Seven: The Coat that didn't Belong.................... *69*
Chapter Eight: The Fear That Wore a Mask *80*
    Anna – The Archivist's Thread (Present Day) 91
    Anna – The First Life (Unknown Era) 93

Chapter: 10: The Keeper... *97*
Chapter Eleven: Threads Yet to Be Told......................... *101*
Chapter Twelve: The Ink That Never Dried *103*
Chapter Thirteen: The Life That Hasn't Happened Yet.. *108*
Chapter Fourteen: David – The Thousand Lives............. *113*

Chapter Fifteen: The Girl of Tongues *118*

Chapter Sixteen: The Coal Dust Dreamer *121*

Chapter Seventeen: The Weight of Stone *126*

Chapter Eighteen: The Silence Beneath the Floorboards 129

Chapter Nineteen: The Bones of the Earth *133*

Chapter Twenty: The Enchanted Mirror – A Life Remembered *139*

Chapter Twenty One: The Boy Who Carried a Century of Fear *143*

Chapter Twenty Two: The One Who Knew His Name *148*

Chapter Twenty Three: The Keeper's Return *152*

Chapter Twenty Four: The First Silence *156*

Chapter Twenty Five: The Echo in Your Hands *161*

   The Book of Echoes *162*

   The Enchanted Spectacles *162*

   The Coat of a Thousand Lives *163*

   Final Reflection *165*

Dedication *168*

Coming In 2025 .... *169*

THE HEART BEHIND THE WORDS

About the Author:

My name is Geoffrey Loveday, and like you, I walk a path shaped by growth, remembrance, and a desire to make meaning of it all.

Yes, I've written nine books. Yes, I hold professional titles and credentials. But what truly defines me is not found in a list of achievements. It's found in the quiet, persistent call to write, to create something that speaks to the soul. I don't always know where this calling comes from, only that it is ancient, insistent, and undeniably alive within me.

I do not write because I have all the answers. I write because something inside me knows that truth, real, human truth, is worth sharing. That healing begins with honesty. That stories, when shared from the heart, have the power to reconnect us with ourselves and with each other.

My work is not about fixing people. It's about helping them remember who they've always been beneath the noise, beneath the inherited wounds, the conditioning, the pain.

Through The Loveday Method and Inherited Therapy, I offer pathways back to wholeness, not as a saviour, but as a fellow traveller who's learned to begin again.

As a certified hypnoanalyst, clinical hypnotherapy instructor, and guide to thousands of transformational journeys, I've seen profound change unfold; not through force, but through gentle remembering.

The real magic happens when people reconnect with their own truth, their own power, and finally come home to themselves.

I don't claim to be special. But I do know, deeply and without doubt, that what I carry is meant to be shared.

This is my offering. And it is given with the hope that it reaches those who need it most.

Dedication:

This book is a love letter to the remarkable souls who have shaped my life with their quiet strength, boundless wisdom, and enduring love. You are etched into every part of who I am. Your impact, profound, sacred, and lasting, lives in me, guiding me through every chapter of this journey.

To my father, your calm presence and unwavering love still echo through my days. Though I can no longer hear your voice, I feel your guidance in every decision, your steadiness in every storm. In your silence, I've discovered the power of a love that never fades, a love that still steadies me when the world shifts.

To my mother, our time was too brief, yet your light continues to shine in me. You taught me the fragile beauty of life, and with that, the courage to hold onto what matters most. In every gentle moment, every act of care, I feel your spirit beside me.

To my grandparents, aunts, and uncles, your stories are stitched into the fabric of who I've become. You gave me a sense of belonging, a legacy of kindness and grace.

Your love was the first home I ever knew, and it still grounds me.

To Alma and Leon, my in-laws, your warmth and open hearts welcomed me with more love than I could have hoped for. Your quiet generosity has enriched my life in ways that words alone cannot convey.

To my beloved wife, though your earthly presence is gone, your love continues to shape my world. I feel you in the laughter of our children, in the stillness of early morning, in the strength you left behind. Your faith in me fuels every word I write. You remain a part of everything I am and everything I do.

To our children, you are my purpose, my strength, my endless source of wonder. You've shown me that love endures, expands, and even deepens in the face of life's hardest truths. Through your hearts, I see all the goodness this world still holds.

To my grandchildren, your joy is my light, your innocence a reminder that hope is always within reach. You carry forward the love and legacy of those who came before you, and in you, the future feels bright and beautiful.

To my sons-in-law, thank you for standing with us, not just as family by name, but as family by spirit. Your character, your kindness, your respect enrich this circle we hold dear.

To my brothers, your absence is a quiet ache that never leaves, yet your memory is a well of strength I draw from constantly. I hear your laughter in my mind, feel your pride in my heart. You are with me still, in every breath, in every step forward.

To my dear friends, mentors, and companions on this path, your belief in me carried me through. Your love, your wisdom, your unwavering presence have been lifelines in times of both darkness and light. I could not have come this far without you.

This book is for all of you. Every word is infused with your love, your courage, your influence. You are the heartbeat behind these pages, the reason they exist. From the depths of my soul, thank you, for walking beside me, for lifting me, for loving me. Always.

Inspiration:

This book is a tribute to the extraordinary resilience of those walking through illness with bravery, grace, and determination. Whether you are fighting, healing, or still finding your way, this is for you. Your courage has left an indelible mark on me, and your stories continue to inspire countless others.

To those who have generously shared their journeys: thank you. In your vulnerability, you've shown us the power of perseverance and the strength that grows in life's most uncertain moments.

To the healthcare professionals and researchers, your commitment to healing and discovery offers hope where it's needed most. Your work doesn't just treat illness; it transforms lives.

To the families, caregivers, and loved ones who stand beside those in need: your quiet strength and constant support are forms of love that speak louder than words. You've touched not only this book but my heart.

To the organisations and foundations that advocate, educate, and uplift, your tireless efforts are a lifeline. Your mission changes lives in ways numbers and statistics can never fully measure.

To my readers: your openness and empathy are the threads that connect us. By engaging with these stories, you help create a space for understanding, connection, and healing.

And to those behind the scenes, my mentors, editors, and unwavering supporters, your faith in this project brought it to life. Thank you for every encouraging word, thoughtful critique, and moment of belief.

This book is more than pages and ink. It's a celebration of human strength, compassion, and the unyielding will to keep going. Thank you for being part of it.

Why I write this:

When I was young, sport came effortlessly – cricket, football, anything I tried. I moved like someone born for it. People praised my skill, and saw a bright path ahead.

But each time it mattered – each trial, each moment of chance – something slipped. Something closed. An injury, a silence, a turn of fate. It was as though the universe itself said: this is not for you.

And for years, I thought I had failed.

Until I began to wonder: did I choose this path before I arrived here? Had I mapped my life from somewhere beyond, planting lessons like seeds in the dark?

Even as a child, I was called an old soul. I felt things others didn't. I knew sorrow before I knew words. I carried dreams that didn't seem mine. And still, I never imagined the road I walk now – hypnotherapist, guide, author of ten books.

It doesn't feel like I write them. It feels as if I remember them. As if something ancient is speaking through me.

These stories – these lives held within the coat – are not inventions. They are fragments of truth, stitched into fiction. They are echoes of lives still breathing through ours.

They remind us why we grieve what we've never lived. Why we flinch at shadows that aren't ours? Why do some dreams feel like memories?

We are not haunted. We are being handed something. Something to finish. Something to forgive. Something to remember.

If you feel something stir as you read, if you've always felt a pull toward the unseen – perhaps you are not just reading this book.

Perhaps it's reading you. Let us keep going. Let us remember together.

"The Soul Remembers", by Geoffrey Loveday

(Creator of The Loveday Method® and Inherited Therapy)

You may open this book and call it fiction.

But I invite you, before you turn another page, to pause. To ask yourself "What if the stories you are about to read are not imagined, but remembered?"

Because what if you haven't stumbled onto this book by accident? What if something inside you, something older than your name, led you here?

My name is Geoffrey Loveday. For over thirty years, I have worked with those who suffer in silence. People weighed down by invisible burdens. By depression, anxiety, or grief that feels too large to explain.

And over time, I discovered something remarkable. These feelings don't always begin in this life.

In my work, I've guided people into their subconscious, not to analyse, but to remember. And what they found was extraordinary.

Lives before this one. Memories not from childhood, but from centuries long past. Emotions passed down through generations, like echoes vibrating through time. These aren't fantasy. They are the soul truth.

And The Loveday Method® is the path inward.

These stories - the Coat of a Thousand Lives, the Book of Echoes, the Enchanted Spectacles, and the Akashic Library - are drawn from the real journeys I have taken people on.

Some met themselves as midwives persecuted for healing. Others as soldiers were silenced by guilt. Still others remembered futures not yet lived. And each time, something changed.

The anxiety faded. The depression lifted. The pain made sense. Because the soul was no longer whispering, it was finally being heard.

You may still choose to call this fiction. But I ask you to consider something else. What if you are already living a story that began long before you were born?

What if the fear you feel is a message, not a flaw?

What if the sadness that comes from nowhere belongs to someone who once lived, and who now waits for you to set them free?

These are not just tales to entertain. They are doorways.

You may laugh. You may cry. You may feel an ache you cannot explain. That's how you know the remembering has already begun.

So now, take a breath. Open your heart. And let us begin the journey;

Back to where the soul first spoke. Back to the moment it all began.

But if you're still holding this book in your hands, if your heart stirred during one of the echoes, if something you couldn't explain pulled you back to read more, then

I must gently offer this: You were never just reading, you were remembering.

You see, some of us do not come here to simply live. We come carrying threads. Threads of sorrow that do not begin in this lifetime. Threads of knowing we never learned but somehow always knew. Threads of dreams we could not name, and griefs we could not explain.

And when a thread begins to hum, a soft vibration in the background of life, you don't always know where it leads. Until it leads you here.

To this page. To this breath. To this quiet remembering.

There is a word for those who feel like this. For those who remember without knowing why. For those who walk through life with one foot still somewhere else.

They are called **The Threads of the Forgotten**.

What are the Threads of the Forgotten?

They are not a religion. They are not a secret society. They are not chosen by ceremony or bloodline. They are born through remembering.

The moment you recognise a pain that never belonged to you, and you choose to heal it anyway; the moment you sit in silence, and the silence speaks back in echoes; the moment you realise your dreams might be memories, and your thoughts are sometimes not your own, that is when you begin the path. You are one who follows the thread.

Through lifetimes unseen, through bodies borrowed like pages in an ever-turning book, through dreams that were never dreams at all, but glimpses, whispers, truths wrapped in silence, the Thread finds you.

It does not shout. It does not rush. It hums. Softly. Steadily. Pulling you not forward, but inward. Toward the thing you have always carried but never quite named.

It winds through the ache behind joy. Through the question behind knowing. Through the longing behind breath.

And then, when the moment is right, it begins to unravel.

Not to fall apart, but to reveal.

Through The Loveday Method, you have walked these echoes. You've followed memory not with your mind, but with your heart. You've touched the seams of time itself through the weight of the Coat, through the pages of the Book of Echoes, through the vision of the Enchanted Spectacles, and what you saw there wasn't just a story.

It was you. The deeper you. The one who has done this before. Not once. Not twice. But across ages and civilisations, beneath pyramids and inside orphanages, as healer, seeker, soldier, mother, outcast, and child.

You have crossed these thresholds again and again, each time forgetting just enough to make the remembering sacred.

You've spoken in forgotten tongues. You've carried burdens that were never yours. You've died with your song still in your chest, and yet, here you are again. Alive. Awake. Aware.

And now, in this lifetime, with this breath, in this sacred moment between the seconds...

Ready to remember not who you've been, but who you were always meant to become.

Because the Thread does not lead you back. It leads you home.

Somewhere behind your story, woven between your quiet ache and your brightest gift, is The Coat of a Thousand Lives.

You may not have seen it. Not with your eyes. Not in the waking world. But perhaps you've felt it...

A hush in the air just before you speak something true. A flicker in your chest when you walk into certain rooms. The sensation that someone is watching, not with fear, but with recognition.

As if something older than memory is reaching toward you with invisible hands.

That is the Coat calling.

Not made of fabric. Not stitched with thread. But spun from the essence of lives once lived, each strand humming with echoes of what still matters.

Worn by seers and seekers, healers and hollowed-out kings, it has crossed empires, survived fire, waited in shadows, and carried the breath of forgotten generations within its folds.

And now it is calling you.

You may feel it when you least expect it, in a dream that lingers too long, a breeze that chills you on a still summer night, a feeling in your bones that you are not only you, but someone else too. Someone ancient. Someone watching through the window of your life, with quiet eyes and a half-remembered name.

Because once worn, even once, you are never the same.

The Coat does not just wrap around you. It weaves you in. You become part of the Thread. Part of the remembering. Part of the unseen story walking through time.

And the Coat?

It waits in the spaces between your doubts. It waits in silence after the question. It waits in the breath before your yes.

If you listen closely, you may hear it rustling now. Calling you. Not to become something new, but to remember what you've always been.

A keeper of lives. A bearer of echoes. A soul wrapped in time. And the Coat remembers you.

This is a story that must be told

How The Loveday Method Brought One Man Back from the Edge of Life

This is more than a story. It's a testimony. A quiet miracle, made possible by presence, precision, and something deeper: a remembering of the soul.

Let's go back to 2018. We'll call him David.

David had reached a place most people only glimpse in their nightmares. He wasn't just sad, he was drowning in darkness. A silence so complete, he believed there was no way out.

One night, he stood on the edge of a building. Ready to jump. But just before he let go, a single thought interrupted:

What if I survive? What if I don't die—but live, broken, trapped?

That fear stopped him. It saved him. But only for a while.

A year later, the darkness had grown stronger. This time, he bought a rope. Drove to a secluded place. Tied the noose. Climbed the tree.

And then something impossible happened.

A stranger appeared. A man walking his dog on a route he never took. In his pocket... a Stanley knife. He said later, "I saw it on the kitchen table this morning. Something told me to take it. I thought I'd just toss it back in the toolbox later."

He climbed the tree and cut the rope, saving David's life.

Call it coincidence. Call it fate. But that interruption was only the beginning.

A few days later, David was given a phone number. A friend said, "Just call. Once." So he did.

We spoke, and I listened. Truly listened.

Then came our first session together using The Loveday Method. And in that sacred space, something opened.

David met his grandmother. She had been gone for years, yet he saw her. Felt her arms. Smelled her perfume. He sobbed as her memory wrapped around him, not as an idea, but as a presence.

Then he saw his first birthday. His mother holding him. Not a memory, but an experience. He wasn't imagining it. He was returning.

What is The Loveday Method?

It's not hypnosis. It's not talk therapy. It is a guided, heart-centred journey, gently excavating the soul's memory. Not to fix, but to restore. To bring people back to who they were before the pain.

It's not about suggestion. It's about remembering.

Clients step into a space where time folds. Where the body reveals what words cannot. Where healing becomes felt, not forced.

David had five more sessions. Each one deeper. Each one lighter. He remembered joy. Moments of beauty hidden beneath the rubble.

Four years later, he told me: "I can still feel her hug. I don't understand it. I just know it was real."

When he told his mother what he saw, details she'd never shared, she wept.

He had remembered the unseen. And in doing so, he found his reason to live.

Today, David is not just alive. He is free.

This story is not fiction. It is living proof that some wounds are older than our names. That suffering is inherited. But so is healing.

That memory is not bound by time. That love, real, soul-rooted love, can cross lifetimes.

And that somewhere, in silence, the coat is waiting still.

Coat of a Thousand Lives

A coat that, when worn, becomes a vessel through time, reliving a life intertwined between the past and the present.

Long before ink met parchment, before stars were named and songs were sung, there was a Coat, not crafted by hand, but born from the loom of time itself. It was said to be the First Thread.

Woven from the signs of forgotten souls and stitched with strands of lost yesterdays, the Coat of a Thousand Lives passed silently through centuries, a vessel of remembrance, a key to lives once lived binding the past to the present like a seam unseen.

To wear it was to become not only oneself, but also those whose echoes still lived in the threads. Time would fold. Moments long buried would bloom again. And the wearer would walk between then and now.

But the Coat was only the beginning.

When the world grew louder, when memory faded into myth, there came The Book of Echoes, a sentient tome whispered into existence by the final breath of a timekeeper. Its pages would write themselves in the presence of truth, recording the footsteps of those who dared to cross the veils of history.

And later, from the well of moonlight and mirrors, emerged the Enchanted Spectacles lenses through which the bearer could see what others had felt, feared, and forgotten. Not just visions, but full emotions, layers of time worn thin by understanding.

Together the Coat, the Book, and the Spectacles formed a triad of relics known only to a few: The Threads of the Forgotten. Wanderers. Witnesses. Keepers of the Unlived.

Their stories are hidden, but if you listen closely, in the silence between seconds, you might hear the soft rustle of fabric, and remember.

The Beginning: The Return of the Hidden Ones

"The Universe never forgets. It only waits for you to remember."

Long before the first books were bound, before the first candle lit the dark, before time itself had settled into hours and years, there were whispers. And within them, power.

The ancients did not write as we write. They wove threads of memory, wisdom, and soul into relics that could travel without moving.

They knew one thing above all: Pain is not bound by time. Neither is healing.

And so they created tools, living tools, not to command, but to awaken. Each one carried a different vibration, a doorway into truth.

- **The Book of Echoes;** a sentient script that writes only in the presence of remembrance.
- **The Enchanted Spectacles;** through which you see not with eyes, but with soul.

- **The Crystal of Alignment**; a silent conductor of memory's frequency.
- **The Coat of a Thousand Lives**; woven from the first thread ever spun.
- **The Lost Key**; for no door that matters opens with reason alone.
- **The Akashic Library**; hidden in the folds of time itself, containing every life ever lived, or imagined, or still to come.

Together, they were guardians of the thread. But humanity forgot.

As greed grew louder, as knowledge became power instead of purpose, the ancients made a vow.

They would hide what we had not yet earned. They would protect what we no longer honoured. Until one came who would walk not for glory, but for truth.

Some say it began with a dream. Others believe it began with loss. But however it started, he remembered.

His name was Loveday. Whether that was his birth name or his echo is unclear. What is clear is this: He felt the Coat before he ever saw it. He dreamt of the Spectacles before he touched them. He heard the Book before he opened it.

He did not invent a method. He reawakened a path. The Loveday Method is not a therapy. It is an ancient inheritance, wrapped in modern breath.

It is how we find our way back to what was taken from us, or what we gave away when we forgot to listen.

And now, in this moment, as the world grows noisier than ever, the relics return.

You may find them not in temples, but in dreams. In flashes of memory that don't belong to this lifetime. In fear you cannot name. In longings that feel older than your skin.

Because the thread has begun to hum. And it knows your name.

So if you find yourself drawn to the Book, if you feel a shiver when you see the Coat, if your palms tingle at the idea of stepping into memory, you are not imagining it. You are remembering it.

The hidden ones never left. They were waiting for you. And now that you've opened this book, the journey has already begun.

Chapter One: "The Scribe's Silence"

Isaac had always feared speaking in public. His words caught like stones in his throat. Meetings made his palms sweat. His voice would vanish, choked by something invisible, ancient. He had no story to explain it. Only a fear too sharp to name.

Until the day the Coat found him.

Tucked behind the counter of a crumbling bookshop tucked into a forgotten alleyway in Florence, its lining shimmered oddly under the dust. "Old cloth," the shopkeeper muttered, shrugging. "It's always been here. No one ever notices it."

But Isaac did. And when he drew it around his shoulders, the world didn't spin. It shifted.

17 October, 1436 | Abbazia di San Spirito | Florence

He blinked. No longer standing in the bookshop, he was seated at a long wooden table, hunched over parchment, the scent of ink and tallow thick in the air.

His fingers, trembling, were stained with ink. His back ached from hours bent in transcription. Candles flickered low. Outside the stained-glass windows, the sun was setting behind the tiled rooftops of Florence.

He was no longer Isaac. He was Brother Tomas, a quiet, observant monk and scribe in service to the abbey. And he had not spoken a word in five years.

The room was silent except for the scratch of quills and the occasional murmured Latin prayer. Monks moved like shadows through the scriptorium, their faces pale and gaunt; their eyes wary.

Brother Matteo sat beside him, carefully copying the pages of an ancient text, Corpus Hermeticum. The teachings of Hermes Trismegistus, heretical by the Church's decree, yet too precious to be destroyed. They copied in secret, knowing discovery could cost their lives.

"Tomas," Matteo whispered once, voice barely audible. "They say the Inquisitors are close. We must finish the folios by All Souls' Day. The others are afraid."

Isaac-Tomas said nothing. He dipped his quill and continued.

Later, as night fell and the bells tolled vespers, Tomas walked the cloister garden, his cowl drawn low. He passed Brother Leon, who paused beside the olive tree where they once used to talk, before the fire, before the betrayal.

"Tomas," Leon said softly, placing a hand on his shoulder. "You haven't spoken since Luca."

Isaac's heart pounded. He remembered, not just as Tomas, but as himself. Luca. His dearest friend. The one who stood at the pulpit and spoke words of light and knowledge. The one who questioned the Church's silences.

The one they burned.

Tomas had been there. He'd watched. He'd said nothing. His silence had saved his life, and haunted every breath since. That night, he dreamed.

He stood in the courtyard again, the flames high, Luca bound and trembling. The crowd shouting "heretic." Luca looked to him, directly into his soul, and did not beg. Only said, "Remember."

And Isaac-Tomas did. He woke in his cell before dawn, heart racing, sweat on his brow. He walked to the small chapel while the others slept and lit a single candle.

And for the first time in years, he spoke. To no one in particular. To the silence itself.

"I remember."

His voice cracked. His hands shook. But something opened.

In the days that followed, he began to speak again. First in prayer, then in conversation. Then, finally, to Matteo, who embraced him with tears.

"Your voice," Matteo whispered, "it sounds like sunlight."

And Isaac realized; his voice had never been broken. It had simply been buried. In terror. In guilt. In memory.

Isaac awoke in the present. Still in the bookshop. Still holding the Coat. His heart pounded, but this time it was not with fear, but with clarity.

His silence wasn't weakness. It was a story. A life that wasn't this one, but had shaped it all the same. And now he could let it go. Because the Coat does not just bring memories. It brings freedom.

Chapter Two: "The Midwife's Fire"

Lila had always feared childbirth.

She couldn't explain it. She wasn't a mother, wasn't even planning to be one. But when her sister fell pregnant, Lila began to panic. She would wake sweating in the middle of the night, images of blood and screaming caught in her throat.

Hospitals made her tremble. The smell of antiseptic made her feel faint. No doctor had answers. No therapist could unravel it.

Until the trunk arrived. A worn cedar chest, inherited from her grandmother who had passed only weeks before. Inside: lace gloves, pressed violets, a bundle of yellowed letters and a coat.

Velvet, heavy, forest green with a worn hem and a strange symbol stitched inside the collar: *Vita Memoria* – Life Remembers.

It smelled of herbs and old books. Without knowing why, Lila drew it around her shoulders. And the moment she did, she was not in her flat anymore.

She stood on a dirt path in the grey chill of early spring. Stone houses huddled together beneath a brooding sky. The wind carried the scent of rain and wood smoke.

She looked down. Her hands were calloused. A leather pouch of herbs hung at her waist. Her feet were bare and dusted with soil. She was not Lila. She was Madeleine Durand, midwife of the village of Riquewihr, nestled deep in Alsace, France in 1721.

3 April, 1721 | Alsace, Northern France

A woman screamed.

Madeleine pushed open the wooden door of a stone cottage. The birthing room was dimly lit with candles. A young woman lay on a straw-stuffed mattress, gripping the sheets, her face slick with sweat.

"Marie," Madeleine whispered gently, placing a cloth on her brow. "You are strong. Breathe with me. We are close."

Marie cried out. Her husband stood near the hearth, pale and trembling, hands twisting his hat. The birth was long. Too long.

Madeleine worked swiftly, calming the mother, easing the pain with infusions, coaxing the child into the world. And then, the stillness. The baby, a boy, was silent.

Madeleine rubbed his back. She tried everything. No breath came. Marie's scream cracked through the air like thunder. Madeleine held the tiny body to her chest, tears sliding down her face. "I'm sorry," she whispered, though she did not know to whom.

The husband stared at her in horror. And then the whispers began.

It started with murmurs. "You gave her the wrong herb." "She cursed the child." "Too many babies have been lost since she arrived."

Within hours, the village turned. The priest refused to bless the child's grave. Old women crossed themselves when she passed. And then, one night, a knock at her door.

Three men stood at her door. One with a torch. One with rope. "You will come," said the man with the torch. "The council has made its decision."

No trial. No questions. Just accusations. Witch.

They dragged her to the old field where herbs once grew wild. Where once she gathered healing, they now built a pyre. As they tied her to the stake, Madeleine did not fight. But she did speak.

"I only ever tried to help," she said. "Even when you didn't believe. I loved your children more than my own."

Only one face in the crowd looked away. A young girl, eyes wide with grief and knowing.

Lila gasped. The scent of fire lingered in her lungs as she opened her eyes. She was back in her apartment, on the floor, the Coat still around her shoulders.

She wept; not from fear, but from recognition. The panic she'd felt her whole life around childbirth wasn't irrational. It was a memory. A life carried forward.

She was not afraid of birth. She was afraid of being blamed for what she could not control. And now, the echo had surfaced.

And now, it could be released.

In her journal later, Lila wrote: "We carry memories we never made. We fear wounds we never earned. But once remembered, they no longer rule us."

She would go on to study midwifery. To hold space for mothers in fear. To honour the lineage of women who once healed in silence.

And every time she wore the Coat, she felt the fire again, not as pain, but as power.

Chapter Three: "The Last Flight"

Milo had always feared heights. Not just a tremble on ladders or a lurch in glass elevators. It was deeper, visceral.

His breath would catch, his legs turn to water. Even crossing pedestrian bridges made his chest tighten.

He didn't know where it came from. He'd never fallen. Never been in a crash. But the fear ruled him. It whispered: Don't go up. Don't trust the air. It won't hold you.

Until the night the Coat found him.

Tokyo was humming with rain that night, silver streaks slicing through neon light. Milo boarded the late train home after a shift at the emergency dispatch centre. The car was nearly empty, except for a lone coat folded neatly across the window seat.

Dark charcoal fabric, seamless lines, an emblem stitched into the collar: two wings curled around a compass rose.

No tag. No owner.

It pulsed with something he couldn't name.

He hesitated. Then, drawn by instinct more than logic, he pulled it on. And the world fractured. Wind roared in his ears.

He stood in the cockpit of a sky station, thousands of metres above Tokyo's skyline. Glass wrapped the control centre. Below, the city stretched like a glowing circuit board, cut by sky rails and floating ambulances.

He looked down at his hands, gloved, steady, and strong. His reflection shimmered on the control glass. Not Milo.

Kaito Takeda. Lead pilot for the SkyMed Crisis Response Unit.

12 May, 2049 | Future Tokyo

The city was in chaos. A cascading power surge had knocked out a third of the energy grid. Elevators failed. Smart-lights blacked out. Traffic above and below ground froze.

Kaito was directing drone ambulances from the upper platform of Tokyo's tallest tower, the Hana Spire. He barked calm orders to his AI co-pilot.

"Reroute Bravo-7 to Ward Four." "Priority on the paediatric route. The child's vitals are unstable."

There was no time to think, just act. Kaito worked with precision. He had done this before. Many times.

But then a red flash. System override.

One drone, Echo-9, the one carrying the child, disappeared from the map.

"No... no, bring it back," Kaito muttered, fingers flying across the console. "Manual override. Pull it back!"

But the drone didn't respond.

He watched, helpless, as it lost altitude, plummeting down somewhere between Shibuya and Harajuku.

Kaito was never the same. He resigned. Refused reassignment. He visited the child's parents anonymously, stood outside their home once, watching their windows in silence.

The city rebuilt. Systems improved. But Kaito did not recover.

One year later, on the anniversary of the collapse, he returned to the Hana Spire.

The cameras were off. The platform was empty. He stepped to the edge. He didn't leave a note.

Milo came back gasping. The train had stopped, the Coat still around him.

He felt sick, like he'd fallen. Like he'd watched someone else fall and couldn't stop it.

He touched his chest. His breath shook. But the fear... it wasn't of heights.

It was of failing again. Of watching helplessly. Of holding blame that time refused to erase.

Tears welled in his eyes. He whispered aloud, "I see you, Kaito."

In the weeks that followed, Milo felt different. The fear of heights didn't vanish overnight. But it changed. He began going higher; small lifts, rooftop cafés, the sky bridge near Shinjuku.

Each time he felt the panic rise, he remembered Kaito's steadiness. His care. His humanity.

Kaito wasn't a failure. He was a man trying to save lives in a collapsing world.

And Milo, too, was learning that forgiveness sometimes travels through lifetimes, and finds you in the silence after the fall.

Some echoes rise not from what we did, but from what we couldn't change. The path forward is not to forget, but to remember with kindness.

And sometimes, to fly again.

Chapter Four: "The Warning"

Alina feared cities.

Not with a passing discomfort—but with a primal, paralyzing terror. Crowded streets made her stomach churn. She'd collapse in underground stations. Her breath would vanish in grocery aisles. The more concrete, the more noise, the more people, the smaller she became.

Her colleagues called it a severe form of social anxiety. Doctors prescribed pills and gentle exposure therapy.

But the dreams said otherwise.

She saw ashes falling like snow. Deserts where oceans had once been. Buildings drowned beneath vines. And voices whispering stories of Earth in the past tense.

She never told anyone the worst part.

In her dreams, she was never herself. She was someone else, someone who remembered.

The coat came on a Tuesday morning. No sender. No return address. Wrapped in deep green cloth and sealed with black wax.

Inside, a single note on old parchment: "Put this on when you're ready to remember."

She held it for hours before slipping it around her shoulders.

It didn't feel like clothing. It felt like permission.

Light vanished. Wind howled. When it returned, she stood in the middle of a vast silver field beneath a sky tinged lavender. Tall spires rose like coral from the horizon, flickering with embedded solar veins.

She looked down at her hands—darker skin than her own, scarred at the knuckles. Tough from work. A thin silver cuff blinked on her wrist: "Elara Noven – Earth Colony IV."

29 December, 2120 | Earth Colony IV

Earth was gone. What remained were colonies; floating habitats orbiting the sun, scattered settlements on terraformed moons, and domed outposts on fractured Mars. Elara lived in one of the few remaining Earth-based communities. The ground beneath her feet still bore the bones of old cities.

She was an eco-historian, a Keeper. One of the few tasked with remembering. Her job was to tell stories. Not myths. Not legends. But truths. Documented, recorded truths about what went wrong.

She stood in a room of children, their pale eyes wide and distant.

"...before the Rivers Cracked," she was saying, pointing to a faded image, "before the Ocean's Silence, when songs still came from whales…"

The children listened. But most didn't understand. They had never seen rain. They had never felt wind on bare skin.

One boy, no older than eight, raised his hand. "Why didn't they stop it?"

Elara blinked. That was always the question. And one she had no answer for.

Later, Elara wandered the Archive. A cavern of digital tablets and shattered books, she passed by murals, scenes from Earth's past etched with solar ink.

She paused before a wall titled The Final Fires. It showed cities burning. A great exodus. And the last ship lifting off from a coastline swallowed by the sea.

Elara pressed her hand to the mural. And suddenly she wasn't looking at history. She was in it.

The smoke. The heat. The protests turned to riots. The silence of governments as people begged to be saved. She felt the fear again.

The memory wasn't ancient. It was hers. Passed down. Encoded.

Alina opened her eyes back in her apartment. The world felt... quieter.

She looked out the window, at traffic, at crowds, at a city still humming. Not yet fallen. Her fear of people wasn't irrational. It wasn't trauma.

It was a message. She had been named Elara. She had watched the end. And now, she had come back. To warn.

She resigned from her lab. Started speaking publicly about climate trauma. Joined youth movements, not as a leader—but as a witness.

When someone asked her how she knew what would happen, she simply said: "I remember. And you can, too."

Where time touches you, every echo is a thread. Every fear a doorway. Every ache, a hidden invitation to remember, not just who you are, but who you've been. And who you're being called to become.

The Coat doesn't just take you back. It takes you where you're needed most. Sometimes, that's the past. Sometimes, it's the future. Sometimes…

It's both at once.

Chapter Five: "The Temple of the Silent Star"

The first time Mira touched the Coat, she felt nothing.

No flicker. No vision. Just a strange warmth in her palms and the faint scent of myrrh. She almost laughed.

But that night, when she closed her eyes, she dreamed of stars falling into sand. Of a great golden door opening beneath her feet. Of drums echoing across stone.

And when she woke, she was not in her bed. She was barefoot, her skin dark with desert sun, her body clothed in linen robes stitched with silver moons.

763 BCE | Temple City of Eresh'Amun

The year was 763 BCE, and she was no longer Mira. She was Sa'atari, a High Dream-keeper in the Temple of the Silent Star.

The temple stood high above the salt cliffs, carved into rose-coloured stone. Sa'atari's job was not to lead rituals, but to listen to dreams.

She and others like her believed the Divine spoke not through thunder or fire, but through symbols in sleep.

The sick were brought to her. The grieving. The cursed. The shunned.

She would take their hands, look into their eyes, without a word, and close her own. And see.

Not just the surface of their pain, but the moment it began. Sometimes decades ago. Sometimes lifetimes ago.

She would return from the vision trembling, but calm. And offer a symbol. A chant. A path.

Her whispers became legend. Even kings came to kneel in the shadows of her chamber, asking "What dream am I trapped inside?"

Mira watched it all unfold, wide-eyed inside Sa'atari's body, the smells of saffron and oil, the cool rush of palm fronds brushing stone walls.

She could feel Sa'atari's heartbeat like her own. And she could feel what came next. The temple was dying.

Not from war. But from silence. A new ruler had risen. A young king obsessed with order, who outlawed dream interpretation as "madness."

He sent soldiers to the Temple of the Silent Star. To burn the scrolls. To shatter the starlit mirrors. They came at night.

Sa'atari didn't run. She stood before them, robes glowing under the moon. When they demanded she denounce her gift, she looked into the captain's eyes and simply said "You fear the dream because you've already seen your end in it."

That night, she was taken. But not before she whispered one last message to a trembling novice.

"What is forgotten in one age will be remembered in the next. Dreamers do not die. They wait."

Mira returned to herself gasping. Tears fell silently, not from sadness, but from knowing.

Her lifelong fear of sleep, the paralysis she'd battled for years, was not trauma. It was a memory. The soul's warning. A vow broken once before.

But now she could rewrite it.

She began sleeping with intention. She recorded dreams. She began helping others interpret theirs.

And one day, a young girl came to her, eyes wide with fear.

"I keep dreaming of stars falling into sand," the girl whispered. "And a woman who says the dreams aren't lies."

Mira took her hand. And the cycle began again.

Not all memories are pain. Some of it is power waiting to be reclaimed.

And through the Coat, Mira had remembered not just who she'd been, but who she had always been becoming.

The dreamer. The listener. The guide.

Because the wisdom of the soul is not lost. It is simply waiting for us to close our eyes and return.

Chapter Six: Sarah - The First Thread

Sarah had not meant to return. Not to the old house. Not to the attic. Not after the funeral. But something in the stillness of her grandmother's home called to her. Maybe it was grief. Maybe it was guilt. Maybe it was the echo of a name she could no longer say without pain; Clara.

Her best friend. Her near-sister. Gone.

Sarah found the coat folded carefully in a cedar chest beneath a drape of linen. Heavy wool. Rough seams. Timeless. She didn't remember it from childhood, and yet it felt familiar. Like something she'd been waiting for.

When she slipped it on, the attic fell away. The air changed.

1872 | Rural England

Gone was the dim dust of afternoon. In its place, the crisp scent of wood smoke, the bite of winter, the golden hush of early morning in another century.

She was barefoot. The floor was not floorboards, but cold stone. The walls were thick, plastered, and low.

And when she looked down—her hands were smaller. Paler. A ribbon of soot streaked one wrist.

Then a voice called: "Jane!"

Sarah turned, heart hammering. The name clung to her skin like dew. She ran to the window, pulling back a muslin curtain. A man in a black coat crossed the street, tipping his hat to her.

"Morning, Miss Jane," he said with a nod, as if he knew her well. Sarah managed a smile, though her heart pounded. She didn't know him, but Jane did.

Outside, horses clopped past. A cart of hay creaked by. Chimneys puffed smoke into a pink dawn sky.

She wasn't watching history. She was inside it.

Over the next hours - or days, it became hard to tell - Sarah lived Jane's life; a girl on the edge of womanhood, brimming with secrets and sorrow.

Jane sang to the fire when no one was listening. She wrote letters she never sent. She dreamed of a boy she would never marry. And she feared something, deeply; a shadow in the night, a truth never spoken aloud.

Sarah felt it all. The ache of it. The small joys. The weight of silence. But the memory that shook her came on the third night:

A scream. A barn aflame. Running. Smoke clawing her lungs.

She woke gasping, sweat-soaked, as if the fire had licked her own skin. She was not lost. Only waiting to be remembered.

The voice, Jane's voice, was everywhere now. In the creak of the stairs. The hush of the wind.

Sarah followed the thread. Piece by piece. She learned that the fire was no accident. Jane had known something. Had tried to stop it. Had failed.

And Sarah began to see herself in Jane. Another girl who had seen the signs and turned away. Who had let silence become a coffin.

To save Jane, Sarah would have to do what she never did for Clara; speak, act, listen, and REMEMBER.

When the coat finally pulled her back, she was standing in the attic once more. But she was not the same.

She touched the wool at her chest and whispered, "Not by changing the past, but by learning how to carry it forward."

And the coat, hanging on its wooden form, shimmered quietly in agreement.

Later, in her dreams, she would see a woman's face she did not recognise, a wartime painting, eyes defiant. The name "Adele" would drift across her sleep like smoke.

That night, Sarah couldn't sleep. Not after the gallery. Not after seeing Adele's eyes staring back at her from the canvas, eyes she now realised had once looked out through her own.

The street outside was quiet. Paris hushed beneath a pale moon.

She sat by the hotel window, the coat folded across her lap. Her fingers traced the seams, the edges, and the worn velvet at the collar.

She whispered the name again: "Adele."

The memory came; not as a dream, but as something deeper. A presence. A pressure behind her ribs.

She remembered the stone floors. The echo of boots in the alley. The cold bite of shame when no one would meet her gaze.

She had lived Adele. And Adele had lived a silence not unlike her own.

But Adele had written. Had painted. Had stood in the square with her head held high while the world tried to turn its back.

Sarah pressed her palm flat to the coat. She had been quiet for too long.

About Clara. About everything.

Adele had given her a gift, not just a glimpse into the past, but permission to speak. To endure. To hold the weight of a truth too long buried.

She stood. Walked to the desk. Took out a sheet of paper. She began to write.

"Clara once told me that silence could be a kindness. I believed her. But now I think silence is just a story left untold. And we owe our stories something more than that."

The coat shimmered softly in the moonlight, and Sarah knew, she wasn't done.

There were more lives in the coat. More truths waiting to be carried forward.

And this time, she would not walk away.

Not again.

Chapter Seven: The Coat that didn't Belong

It was 1920. A time when life, at least on the surface, seemed simpler. But beneath the jazz and gentility, some souls carried storms they couldn't name.

John was one of them.

By all appearances, he had everything he needed; a steady job at the rail station, a modest flat, polished shoes, and a pocket watch inherited from his father.

But inside, he felt lost. Like he was watching his own life from across the room. As if the days belonged to someone else. A quiet ache followed him, not sharp, but constant.

He had no words for it. People didn't talk about such things back then. Depression wasn't a word they used. You were just "melancholic," or "ungrateful." But John wasn't ungrateful.

He was simply out of place. A soul misplaced in time.

It started one autumn morning. John opened his wardrobe to find a coat he didn't recognise. Long, dark, heavy wool, military-style, but older. Too elegant for the war he had just returned from.

He frowned. Checked the label. There wasn't one. And yet, when he touched it, his fingers trembled.

A scent rose from the fabric. Wood smoke. Saddle leather. Something ancient.

He pulled it on hesitantly, and in that moment, the thread pulled tight. Images flooded him. Not dreams; memories.

Galloping on horseback across snow-covered fields. A woman in a velvet shawl weeping in candlelight. The weight of command. The shame of betrayal. A life that felt more like his than the one he was actually living. He dropped to his knees. Breath caught. Heart pounding. For a moment, he wasn't John.

He was Aleksandr, a cavalry officer in 18th-century Russia, disgraced after a secret uncovered, banished from everything he loved.

And he had died with regret in his chest. Regret that had passed down, waiting, until now.

John didn't know the words for what was happening. He didn't know he was part of a greater memory. That what he was feeling wasn't madness, but the echo of a soul left unfinished.

And the coat? It wasn't just fabric. It was a trigger. A relic. A tether between lives.

He would soon find the spectacles. He would soon meet a guide. And when he did, everything would change.

The next morning, John awoke feeling heavier, as if the memories from the day before had curled up in his chest and refused to leave.

He stood in the mirror, staring at the coat. It still hung neatly on the hook where he'd placed it. It hadn't moved. It hadn't changed. But somehow, it was watching him. Not with eyes, but with a presence.

He didn't wear it again. Not yet. But the images it brought wouldn't stop.

That day at the station, everything felt off. The rhythm of the trains, usually so comforting, was jagged. The way people moved, their clothes, their laughter, felt wrong. He caught himself looking for horses. Listening for Russian.

It was around three o'clock, just after the eastbound train left, when he appeared. An older man. Well-dressed, sharp blue eyes. But it wasn't his appearance that struck John, it was the feeling.

Like the man knew him. Knew something about him. Not in a suspicious way. But in a way that felt ancient.

"You've worn it, haven't you?"

The man approached slowly, hands behind his back. He didn't offer a name. Didn't introduce himself.

He simply said, "You've worn it, haven't you?"

John blinked. "I'm sorry?"

"The coat. The one that doesn't belong to this life."

A chill ran through him. He hadn't told anyone. Not a soul.

"I know how it feels," the man continued. "Like stepping into a memory that isn't yours, but somehow, it is."

John said nothing. The station blurred around them. "There's a name for what you're experiencing," the man said gently. "A way to understand it. It's called The Loveday Method."

The man handed him a small card—ivory parchment, almost warm to the touch. Embossed in gold:

> The Loveday Method,
> For those who carry what time has forgotten.
> Ask for G. Loveday

"You may not believe in it now," the man said. "But you will. Because the past doesn't sleep forever. And you've just begun to wake up."

He tipped his hat and walked away. Gone before John could ask a single question.

That night, the dreams returned. Not Aleksandr's this time. But something deeper, older. Like flickers from many lifetimes calling his name.

And in the silence between heartbeats, he heard the whisper, "Find him. Find the one who remembers. Loveday."

John arrived at the address printed on the ivory card. It was a townhouse, tucked quietly between a row of identical buildings in Bloomsbury. Nothing about it looked unusual. But as soon as he stepped through the doorway, the air changed.

It was quieter here. Heavier, too. Not oppressive, just sacred.

A tall man with calm eyes greeted him with a warm, knowing smile. He didn't introduce himself. He didn't need to.

This was Geoffrey Loveday.

Geoffrey led John into a softly lit room. No clocks. No distractions. Only stillness.

"This won't feel like anything you've ever done before," he said calmly. "But it will feel familiar. Because the soul remembers."

John said nothing. He wasn't sure he even believed any of this. And yet, he was here.

He lay back in the chair, closed his eyes, and Geoffrey's voice began to guide him.

"With each breath," Geoffrey whispered, "you go deeper.
Not away from yourself, but into your true self."

"There's a staircase now. Ten steps. At the top, a door. When you reach it... open it. And trust what comes."

John climbed. One step at a time. And when he reached the top, he opened the door...

And Aleksandr was waiting.

He was on horseback. The cold air stung his face. Snow clung to the trees. He wore the same coat from his wardrobe.

But this wasn't London. This was Russia. His Russia.

He could feel the ache in his hands from holding the reins too tightly. He could smell the leather, the horses, the smoke from distant fires. He could feel the shame lodged deep in his chest.

"I failed them," he said aloud. "My men. My family. I made a choice I thought was honourable, but it cost everything."

Geoffrey's voice gently floated through the memory.

"What was the choice?"

Aleksandr-John clenched his jaw.

"I spared a village. They were meant to be punished, but I couldn't. They called it treason."

John's breath caught in his real-world body. His fingers twitched. A tear slipped from his closed eyes.

"I've carried this guilt all my life, but I never knew where it came from. I've always felt like I betrayed someone."

"Even now, in this life, I never trust my own decisions. I sabotage things before they begin."

And in that moment, he saw it clearly. The echo of Aleksandr's grief was still shaping John's life.

The failure. The guilt. The exile. All of it had passed forward, unhealed. Until now.

"What does Aleksandr need to hear?" Geoffrey asked.

His voice shaking, John replied, "He needs to hear that compassion isn't weakness. That mercy isn't betrayal. He needs to be forgiven. Not by others. But by himself. He made the right choice."

And with those words, the snow began to fall slower. The cold softened. The memory began to lift.

John exhaled. Long. Deep. Like he hadn't breathed fully in years.

When he opened his eyes, he was quiet. But different. Lighter. Like something had been set down.

"It was real," he whispered. "I was him."

Geoffrey simply nodded. He had seen this before. But it never lost its magic.

"That part of you is now free," he said. "And because of that, you are free to live without his shame."

John looked at his hands. He felt them for the first time.

And for the first time in his life, he didn't feel like a stranger in his own skin.

Later, as he walked back into the city streets, John saw the world with new eyes. The coat no longer haunted him. It now felt like something that had served its purpose. A bridge to the truth.

And as he turned the corner onto Woburn Walk, he whispered to no one and everyone, "Thank you, Aleksandr. You can rest now. I'll take it from here."

Chapter Eight: The Fear That Wore a Mask

Some fears have no name. No reason. No explanation. Because they don't begin in this life. They are echoes, buried deep, waiting for the moment you're ready to face them.

It was 1943, and the world was already burning.

Raymond was twenty-six, working as a translator for the British government, helping decode intercepted French messages. His French was flawless. His instincts? Sharper than most. But there was something about him that didn't quite fit the room.

He walked like he was avoiding someone, even when he was alone. He jumped at the sound of bells. He couldn't stand the feel of silk.

"Sends a chill right down my back," he once muttered, brushing his fingers off as if something had crawled over them.

He couldn't explain it. None of it made sense. He wasn't superstitious. He wasn't dramatic. But deep down, he was terrified. Of what, he didn't know.

One afternoon, while sorting through confiscated correspondence, he found a name that stopped his breath: Lucien Delacroix.

Something about it sent a spike of cold through his spine. His hands shook. His vision blurred.

He had no memory of this man. But his body remembered.

That night, he dreamt of flames. Crowds. A wooden stage. And the sound of cheering.

But he wasn't in the crowd. He was on the stage. His hands bound. His heart was pounding. And above him, a blade.

Desperate, and quietly ashamed, Raymond sought out a man whispered about in certain circles, a hypnotist. A "memory man." Someone who helped people see things that couldn't be seen.

That man was Geoffrey Loveday.

Raymond didn't explain much when he arrived. Just that he felt something was wrong. Deeply wrong. And it had nothing to do with the war.

Geoffrey nodded, as if he'd been expecting him all along.

Under trance, Raymond's breath slowed. His fists unclenched. And the moment Geoffrey asked him to open the door, the past rushed in like a flood.

"Paris," Raymond whispered, "1789."

His voice changed. It was stronger. Sharper. Almost aristocratic.

"My name is Henri. Henri de Montreux. I'm… I'm not safe."

The images tumbled out. He had been a nobleman, not cruel, not corrupt; but marked by his bloodline.

When the revolution came, he tried to protect his staff. He tried to reason with the crowds. But it didn't matter. His name was on a list.

And one day, they came for him. Dragged him through the streets. Laughed as he was paraded in rags. Threw flowers. Spit. Applauded.

"I wasn't afraid of death," he said in trance. "I was afraid of being forgotten. Of dying a villain in a story I never wrote."

Raymond stirred. His body trembled. Tears slid down his face, unbidden.

"I've always feared being judged," he said, "for something I can't explain. Now I know why. I died misunderstood. I was made a symbol. But I wasn't the man they thought I was."

"I've carried that shame for centuries."

And suddenly, the fear that had followed him since childhood, the fear of being exposed, misread, the fear that somehow he was guilty of something unseen, made sense.

In the stillness, Geoffrey asked one question, "What would you say to Henri now?"

Raymond, his eyes still closed, smiled through the tears.

"You mattered. Your truth mattered. You were not your title. And you are remembered."

In that moment, the blade vanished, the crowd dissolved. And the fear lifted.

When Raymond opened his eyes, he took the deepest breath of his life.

"I don't feel hunted anymore," he said.

That week, he returned to work with a presence no one had seen in him before. He started speaking up. Stopped apologising. He wore silk.

He even began writing letters under a pseudonym, letters of history, of memory, of honour restored. And he signed each one "H. de Montreux".

Chapter Nine: Alan - The Forgotten Orders

His name was Alan.

The year was 1960, but his nightmares belonged to another time.

Since childhood, Alan had seen things that didn't belong to him. He dreamed of jungle heat, starvation, the metallic taste of fear. Japanese prison camps. Torture. Men dying beside him, whispering for home.

He woke up screaming more nights than not. Doctors called it anxiety. He called it a curse.

Even as the dreams faded with age, one thing remained; he couldn't bear enclosed spaces.

Crowded lifts, locked doors, windowless rooms; they triggered a terror he couldn't name. His relationships cracked under the weight of it. His wife no longer reached for his hand in the dark. His son feared the outbursts he couldn't explain.

He felt trapped in his own skin.

But Alan had always loved history. He spent his days on archaeological digs, searching for stories buried beneath the earth; lives long gone, but not forgotten.

It was during a brief trip to an old colonial guest house in the countryside, booked as part of a university excavation that everything changed.

That night, the room was quiet. The bed sheets crisp. The air still. Alan fell into a heavy sleep.

He woke to a glow. A faint shimmer in the corner of the room. He rose, heart pounding. At first, he thought it was a trick of light; moonshine through cracked shutters.

But no. There it was. A coat. Woollen. Tattered. Stained with something darker than age. And glowing faintly, like breath on glass.

He couldn't look away. He reached out. Touched the fabric. And the world fell.

1942 | Burma, Southeast Asia

When he opened his eyes, the heat hit him first. Thick, choking. Wet with rot.

His wrists were bound. Flies crawled over open wounds. Men groaned around him. Some did not move at all.

He was barefoot. He was not Alan. He was Ronald, a British commander in Burma. Captured in 1942 by Japanese forces and marched into hell.

There were no rules. No medicine. No food. No mercy.

They worked them till their bones cracked, starved them till they forgot names, beat them for speaking, for breathing, for existing.

Ronald endured. He held men's hands as they died. He buried their dog tags in secret under banyan trees. He whispered their names so they would not be forgotten.

"Don't let me vanish," one had whispered.

But he had. And now, Alan – Ronald – was back. Forced to feel it. To remember it. Not from a distance. Not from a dream. From inside.

When he returned to his body in the guesthouse, it was nearly dawn. He was on the floor, soaked in sweat. The coat lay beside him. Its seams no longer glowing. Just dark. Still. Waiting.

Alan wept. Not from fear. But from recognition.

He had lived a death not his own. A silence too deep to ignore. In the pocket of the coat, he found a note, water-stained and barely legible: "Lt. R. Whitmore. 4th Battalion. No grave. No cross. No words."

Alan stood up. His legs shook. But his mind was clear for the first time in years. He knew why the dreams had come. He knew what claustrophobia meant. It wasn't a curse. It was a memory.

And now, he would find the names. He would write them. He would speak them. So they would never vanish again.

Two months later, Alan visited a military archive in London. While searching through burial records and POW rosters, a name caught his eye: Jakob Whitmore.

A boy listed as a wartime refugee in Europe, transported to a camp in 1942. No record of survival. Alan's breath caught. He remembered David's story. A child. A coat. A drawing.

Whitmore. Not a common name. On impulse, he searched deeper. Another name emerged: Jane Whitmore, reported dead in a fire in 1872. A village girl from Green Hollow.

The coat had not just shown them different lives. It showed them one life. Fractured. Threaded. And maybe, somehow, family.

Alan touched the coat now folded on the chair beside him. It was still. But not silent. He wasn't the only one carrying the weight of the forgotten.

And he knew he wouldn't be the last.

Anna – The Archivist's Thread (Present Day)

Anna Cartwright wasn't looking for ghosts. She was looking for lineage. A historian by training, and a genealogist by trade, Anna had made a quiet career out of reuniting people with their forgotten pasts.

Old soldier medals, family crests, lost journals, she followed names like footprints in dust.

She wasn't sentimental. Until she found the Whitmores.

It began with a request from an elderly client seeking family records tied to Green Hollow, England. A routine search.

But the names kept surfacing. Jane Whitmore. Lt. Ronald Whitmore. Jakob Whitmore.

Different countries. Different centuries. Too many deaths. Too many missing years.

Then came the strangest part; marginal notes in archived letters and war reports:

"She wore a coat, not hers." "The boy spoke of fire, but the barn hadn't burned yet." "He claimed he remembered a war not yet fought."

Anna dismissed it at first. Superstition. Confusion. Until she came across an anonymous manuscript in a London museum archive: The Coat of a Thousand Lives.

The author? Unknown. The pages? Scattered, unfinished.

But the voices — Sarah, Elijah, Lila, David, Alan — each one described the coat. A vessel. A key. A mirror of memory.

Anna felt a chill. And then she found the final entry, unlabelled but carefully folded:

"There will come a historian who sees not just the past, but the thread that binds it. If she wears the coat, she will not travel backward, but inward. She will find the origin. The first life. And the reason we were chosen."

Anna sat very still. She glanced at the coat hanging on her office door. It hadn't been there before.

Anna – The First Life (Unknown Era)

She stood before the coat for a long time. It didn't shimmer this time. Didn't pulse or whisper. It simply waited.

Anna slipped it over her shoulders.

The room tilted. Light shattered. The air spun with dust, salt, and smoke.

And then, silence. When she opened her eyes, the world had changed.

She stood on a cliff, wind in her hair, overlooking a vast and ancient sea. There were no cities. No engines. Only the hush of waves and the distant call of birds.

The sky was richer, darker. The stars were wrong. Older.

She was barefoot. Her clothes hand spun. Her fingers bore ink stains, and a satchel of scrolls hung at her side.

From behind, a voice spoke a name, "Eshara."

Anna turned. The woman who had spoken wore robes of blue and bone, hair threaded with shells.

"Come," the woman said. "The council waits."

Anna, or Eshara, followed, heart pounding. She had gone not backward. But into the beginning. Eshara was the first.

Not of the Whitmores. But of the Recorders; the memory-keepers of her people.

They did not write books. They became them. Each Recorder wore the coat during the ritual of remembrance, stitched with the lives and lessons of the ancestors.

Each wearer added a thread. A sorrow. A truth.

The coat was not magic. It was memory given shape.

Eshara's people lived by it. Died for it.

Now, the elders warned, the threads were unravelling. Too much was forgotten. Too many voices were lost.

A decision had to be made: to bury the coat forever, or send it forward. Out into time. To those who still remembered how to listen.

Anna listened.

She wandered the village. She helped harvest salt from the shore. She laughed with a boy who taught her the constellations.

And in quiet moments, she sat with the coat in her lap, tracing each stitch like a name she hadn't yet learned.

The past was not behind her. It was within her.

Before she returned, the elders gathered once more. "You were not chosen by blood," one said.

"But by the ache," another added. "The ache to remember. And to carry."

When Anna awoke, the office was just as she'd left it. But the coat was no longer on the door. It was wrapped around her.

And in the corner of her desk, freshly written in her own hand, a note: "The first thread was not sorrow. It was love. And the longing not to forget.

Chapter: 10: The Keeper

Anna stood at the window of her small London flat, the coat folded neatly beside her on a wooden chair. Outside, the city buzzed with ordinary life – buses, footsteps, laughter in cafés. None of them knew that time had bent, that history had whispered, that memory had found its vessel.

She had seen too much now to ever return to simplicity. But it was not her burden alone.

She returned to Green Hollow – the place where so many threads began. There, in the village library, she requested a meeting with the local archivist: a young man named James Whitmore.

He had always felt... different. Drawn to old stories. Haunted by vivid dreams he never understood.

When Anna entered the reading room, James stood up. He looked at her as though he'd met her in a dream.

"Have we...?"

"Not yet," Anna said softly. "But you've been waiting."

She placed the coat on the table between them. James stared at it. A pulse flickered beneath his skin – not fear, but recognition.

"What is it?"

Anna smiled gently. "It's yours now. If you choose to wear it."

He hesitated. Then, slowly, reached forward.

The coat shimmered faintly – as if the lives inside stirred to greet him.

Anna turned to go, but paused at the door.

"Remember," she said. "The coat doesn't give answers. It gives memory. What you do with it – that's the legacy."

James nodded, wide-eyed.

As Anna stepped into the street, she felt the wind pick up – soft, like the breath of time passing.

Behind her, a new story was beginning. The coat was no longer waiting. It was moving forward.

As you've turned these pages, stepping into the footsteps of those who wore the coat – Sarah, Elijah, Lila, David, Alan, Anna – I hope something stirred within you. Something deep. Something old.

A recognition.

That we are all connected.

Not just by blood or name, but by memory. By silence. By the ache of stories that were never told, but somehow still live in us.

You may think the tales in this book are fiction. Neatly woven. Impossibly timed.

But I'm here to tell you, they are not. They are echoes. Reflections of lives that once were. Or perhaps still are. The coat is not just a device. It is a witness. A keeper. A call.

Each thread you followed – from the burning barn in 1872 to the jungles of Burma, from secret letters to hidden paintings – is stitched with truth. With the residue of sorrow and memory that binds us across time and silence.

Somewhere, maybe not far from you, someone is having dreams they can't explain. Visions that don't belong to them. A fear they were never taught, but feel all the same.

Maybe it's you.

Chapter Eleven: Threads Yet to Be Told

Let us now journey onward, into stories that lived long before us, and into the pain we still carry today. For in their lives, we may find the roots of our own suffering... and perhaps, the beginning of our healing.

Let us go further. Let us listen deeper.

There are more stories. More lives that once walked this earth long before; lives that still stir beneath the surface, whispering through time.

You may feel them in your quiet moments. You may sense them in your sorrow.

We are not suffering without reason. We suffer because we have inherited wounds that were never healed. We carry echoes of lives that ended in silence, voices stifled, truths buried, griefs dismissed as history.

But they were never just history. They were people. With breath. With fear. With hope.

The girl in 13th-century Spain, accused of witchcraft for dreaming in tongues she had never been taught. The healer in Ghana in 1807, who risked everything to tend to the broken while colonial boots marched closer. The boy in Manchester in 1841, who stitched buttons by moonlight but dreamed of galaxies and drew them in coal dust.

Their suffering was real. Their love was real. And we are still living the consequences, because the world does not forget what it has not faced. We bleed today for what we buried yesterday. But the coat still waits.

Not in museums or myths, but in the quiet corners of those who feel too much, cry without knowing why, dream of places they've never been.

Perhaps you, too, are one of them. And if so, the story is not finished.

It is just beginning. You are not haunted. You are being called. The coat remembers. And it is ready for you.

Chapter Twelve: The Ink That Never Dried

Some echoes are not loud. They live in the hand that hesitates. The thought that disappears before it's spoken. The knowledge we bury to protect the ones we love.

Her name now was Aiko. She lived in Kyoto, worked as a university archivist, and often said she felt more comfortable surrounded by centuries-old documents than people.

Her friends described her as graceful, precise, reserved. She smiled often, but never for long.

Inside, Aiko felt something else. Something is missing. A quiet grief that sat in her bones like a secret.

She had no great trauma in this life. No reason to feel the ache she carried. But for as long as she could remember, she'd dreamt of ink-stained hands, calligraphy scrolls blowing in the wind, and words that were never shared.

"Sometimes I wake up mid-sentence," she said. "As if I was just about to say something important, but I never get to finish."

She found The Loveday Method through a guest lecture in England, a short workshop, more curiosity than calling.

But when she heard the phrase "healing the soul through time", she felt a shift. Not a chill, a homecoming.

She approached Geoffrey quietly after the talk.

"I think I've left something important behind," she said. "And I need to find it."

He looked at her with the soft eyes of someone who knew, who had seen this before, who had once searched for the same thing.

Under trance, her breathing slowed. The room softened. The present dissolved.

"There's mist," she whispered. "Mountains. And a house made of wood and paper."

She was no longer Aiko. She was Mei. A scholar's daughter, living in 11th-century Song Dynasty China. A calligrapher. A quiet genius.

But female.

Which meant her wisdom could only be practiced in secret.

"I wrote at night," she said. "By moonlight. Poetry. Philosophy. Questions too large for the women's quarters."

"My father knew. He taught me. But told me never to let the world know."

"He said, the world does not understand a woman who knows too much."

And so she wrote. Scroll after scroll, hidden beneath the floorboards.

Until the day they were found by a jealous official. A man who'd once courted her, and whom she had refused.

"He called me dangerous," she said, her voice trembling. "Said I mocked the Emperor with my ideas. My words were burned."

"And I was exiled, not to a place, but to silence."

In this life, Aiko had never published. Never shared her ideas aloud. She edited other people's writing with surgical brilliance, but her own voice remained in fragments.

Now, she understood why.

"I was taught that silence is honour," she whispered. "But it was fear, fear of being seen, of being erased again."

Geoffrey asked gently, "What would Mei say now, if she knew she was safe?"

Aiko's breath deepened. Her hands moved in the air, as if writing without paper.

"She would say that truth does not belong to men or women. It belongs to the soul. And she would write again."

After the session, Aiko returned to Japan with something burning in her heart. Not anger. Not sorrow. But permission.

She began writing under the name Mei-Lan a blend of who she was then, and who she is now.

Her essays, on intuition, ancestral memory, and feminine wisdom, began to ripple quietly through academia. Not loud. But impossible to ignore.

And she no longer hesitated.

Because she knew, the words she was born to speak were never truly lost. They had just been waiting.

Chapter Thirteen: The Life That Hasn't Happened Yet

Some echoes don't come from the past. Some are whispers from the future, a calling that hasn't happened, but remembers you anyway.

Her name was Leah. Thirty-two, an artist, a traveller; restless in ways she couldn't explain.

She said she had everything she needed, a stable life, a loving partner, even recognition for her work.

But something inside her refused to settle.

"It's like I'm waiting for something," she told Geoffrey. "But I don't know what. Or who. Or where."

Every night, her dreams showed her the same image, a sprawling city made of glass and light. A high tower. And a coat.

She never saw her face in the dream, only her hands. And they were always wearing the same coat. Long, dark grey, lined with something that shimmered.

She saw herself walking through corridors, guiding others, but not on Earth. At least, not the Earth she knew.

Geoffrey was quiet as he listened. Then simply said: "Some echoes don't come from behind you. Some arrive early because your soul is already walking there."

She agreed to try The Loveday Method. But she didn't want to look back. She asked, "Can I go forward?"

Geoffrey smiled gently. "Wherever your soul is ready to lead, the door will open."

Under trance, Leah stepped through the door. And what greeted her was unlike any life remembered before.

"It's... another planet," she whispered. "But it feels like home."

She described domes of soft metal and gardens grown with sound. A city suspended over the sea, powered by light and breath.

But more than anything, she described her role.

"I guide people through something called 'The Return'. They come to me when they're lost. And I help them remember who they were, before they came here."

"It's like The Loveday Method. But evolved."

She was called Amari. And she wore the coat.

The same coat that once belonged to John. To Aleksandr. And perhaps, even Geoffrey.

Except now it had changed. The lining glowed faintly, embedded with shifting symbols, a living record of all who had worn it.

"I'm not just remembering her," Leah said aloud. "I am her. She's the future version of me. And she's calling me forward."

She paused. "The anxiety I've felt all my life, it's not fear. It's urgency. Because she's already waiting."

When Leah came out of trance, she didn't look disoriented. She looked clear.

She knew her life wasn't behind her. It hadn't even started. Not truly.

"The art I make, it's not random. It's part of the design. Blueprints. Visions. Pieces of what's coming."

She started creating differently. Her canvases changed. They became portals. People cried in front of them. Some said they dreamed of the places she painted, before they ever saw them.

And she no longer questioned it.

The coat, Geoffrey now realised, was not just a relic of the past. It was a marker. A mantle, worn by those chosen to carry the thread.

It had belonged to Aleksandr. It had called to John. It had waited for Leah. And it would, one day, be worn again, by those yet to be born.

Because time does not move in a straight line. It spirals. It folds. And the soul moves through it like wind through silk.

Some echoes don't come from where you've been. They come from where you're meant to go.

And when we stop trying to only heal the past, and begin listening to the future, that's when the whole timeline begins to heal.

Chapter Fourteen: David – The Thousand Lives

David was afraid to sleep.

Every time he closed his eyes, the dreams came. Not dreams. Nightmares.

Barbed wire. Trains groaning through the snow. Muffled crying in the dark. Numbers etched in blue on skin far too young. A child's hand slipping from his.

He wasn't Jewish. He wasn't even raised to believe in much of anything. But the camps haunted him like memories he never lived.

Every night, the same boy – eight, maybe ten – looked up at him as the gates clanged shut.

"Why didn't you help?"

David always woke up gasping, the sound of his own breath choking him.

He tried therapy. Meditation. Wine. Nothing dulled the dreams.

Until the day the coat found him.

It was late. The underground train was nearly empty. He sat in the corner, trying not to think, trying not to feel.

And there beside him lay the coat.

Thick wool. Old buttons. A dark lining that shimmered like ink in water.

He touched it. It was warm. Alive. He didn't think. He slipped it on.

1942 / Germany, WWII

He opened his eyes to snow. To barking dogs. To shouting in German.

He was no longer David. He was small. Hungry. Alone.

A name tag was stitched into his collar:

Jakob.

David was inside the nightmare. But now it was real. He lived it.

Each day, Jakob clung to his mother's skirt. They stood in line for soup that ran out before they reached the front. They slept on wooden planks in a hut that groaned in the wind. In the mornings, Jakob would pretend he wasn't afraid – because his mother needed him to be brave.

There was a girl named Mira who braided the younger children's hair and told stories about butterflies in spring. There was a quiet man who used to be a surgeon, who bandaged fingers with torn sheets and whispered lullabies in Polish.

They were not just part of history. They were people.

They laughed when they could. They shared when they had nothing. They cried when no one was watching.

And then came the list.

Names were called. Jakob's among them.

His mother held him so tightly, he couldn't breathe. "You are loved," she whispered. "Don't forget it."

That night, he dreamed of birds flying over wire.

And then, darkness.

David woke on the floor of his flat, drenched in sweat. The coat was beside him, faintly steaming with the cold of another world.

Inside the pocket was a piece of paper, worn and torn. A drawing in pencil. A boy and a woman. Their hands touching. A yellow star on her chest.

David wept. Not from fear. Not from confusion. From knowing. From remembering.

He didn't return to work that week. Instead, he searched. He found Jakob's name in an old transport list. He found Mira's story in a single sentence buried in a digital archive.

He wrote. Not just what he saw. What he felt.

"If memory is a burden," he wrote, "it is one we carry so they don't have to."

He submitted his manuscript to a publisher. They called it fiction.

But David knew better. It was a life. One of a thousand.

And he would remember them all.

Chapter Fifteen: The Girl of Tongues

Her name was Ysabel, and from the age of seven, she dreamed in languages no one around her understood.

She would wake whispering words that sounded like wind over distant sands or sea-prayers rising from storm-swept shores. Her mother said she was cursed. Her father feared her. The village priest called it possession.

But Ysabel knew the dreams were more than madness. They were memories.

She saw a woman in a marketplace, weaving gold through silk, humming a melody long forgotten. She stood in temples scorched by war, her hands pressing ancient script into clay. She cried over a child lost to plague in a house with no walls.

The coat found her in the winter of her thirteenth year, wrapped around a merchant's relic cart, mistaken for rags. She slipped it on and fell.

Not asleep. But through.

1247 / Spain

She awoke in a quiet mountain village; older, darker, lonelier. The people spoke a tongue she knew, though she had never heard it aloud. She lived as a healer's apprentice, tending the sick and dreaming more clearly than ever before.

But fear followed her. Her gift was not welcomed. Whispers turned to stares.

A fever swept the village. Children died. And when prayers failed, blame sought a name. Ysabel.

They dragged her through the square, her coat torn from her shoulders, her mouth gagged. They called her bruja: witch.

She did not fight. She only whispered a name into the wind. Not hers, someone else's.

When Anna later discovered a scroll buried beneath a ruined chapel – inscribed in five languages, none local to the region – she knew it was Ysabel's final message.

"I was never cursed. I was remembering. Let the next who dreams speak freely. Let her not fear the fire."

Anna wept. Because she remembered the fire. And knew it was not the end.

Chapter Sixteen: The Coal Dust Dreamer

His name was Elias, and he was born with soot under his fingernails.

At nine years old, he worked twelve hours a day in a textile mill, lungs filled with lint and a back hunched from crouching under looms. The clatter of machines was all he knew. The air tasted of oil and sorrow.

He never spoke of dreams. But each night, when the others slept on straw, Elias took a nub of coal and scratched the stars he saw in his mind across the stone wall.

Not constellations he'd learned, but patterns he remembered.

Once, when the overseer caught him drawing instead of sleeping, Elias was beaten so badly he couldn't walk for two days.

But the dreams kept coming.

A telescope aimed at a sky not yet charted. A voice calling him by another name – not Elias, but Samir. A city of domes and scholars. A fire. And hands – his own – closing a book just before the flames took it.

The coat came to him during a snowstorm. Left behind on a hook in the mill yard. Wet wool. Too big. Too strange.

He pulled it on. And fell.

1094 / Córdoba, Southern Spain

He awoke in another body. Older. Taller. His hands ink-stained and calloused from writing. He stood in a study filled with scrolls, astrolabes, and star charts.

He was Samir – a scholar in Córdoba, 1094. A man hunted for the knowledge he preserved.

The city burned around him, but he would not let the maps die. He fled. Hid them beneath floorboards. Passed their patterns on through whispered teachings.

Now Elias remembered them.

He spent weeks in Samir's skin. Felt the same fear. The same defiance. He taught children in secret. He translated the stars for the illiterate. He refused to be erased.

And when the fire came again, he was ready.

Elias woke in the factory shed, trembling. His fingers still traced stars on the wall – but this time, he did not draw them alone.

Other boys came. They watched. They listened. They began to remember too.

Years later, a museum would hang one of his coal sketches beside a plaque that read:

"Anonymous, c.1841 – Thought to be one of the earliest celestial renderings from a child labourer. Based on North African star charts believed lost in the 11th century."

The stars had found their way back.

And so had he.

The coat, folded quietly in a trunk, waited for the next child to feel too small in the world, and dare to dream beyond it.

Let us go further. Let us listen deeper.

There are more stories. More lives that once walked this earth long before us, lives that still stir beneath the surface, whispering through time.

You may feel them in your quiet moments. You may sense them in your sorrow.

We are not suffering without reason. We suffer because we have inherited wounds that were never healed. We carry echoes of lives that ended in silence, voices stifled, truths buried, griefs dismissed as history.

But they were never just history.

They were people. With breath. With fear. With hope.

The girl in 13th-century Spain, accused of witchcraft for dreaming in tongues she had never been taught. The healer in Ghana, 1807, who risked everything to tend to the broken while colonial boots marched closer. The boy in Manchester, 1841, who stitched buttons by moonlight but dreamed of galaxies and drew them in coal dust.

Their suffering was real. Their love was real.

And we are still living the consequences, because the world does not forget what it has not faced.

We bleed today for what we buried yesterday.

But the coat still waits.

Not in museums or myths, but in the quiet corners of those who feel too much, cry without knowing why, dream of places they've never been.

Perhaps you, too, are one of them. And if so, the story is not finished. It is just beginning.

You are not haunted. You are being called. The coat remembers. And it is ready for you.

Chapter Seventeen: The Weight of Stone

Her name was Arina.

In the present, she was an architect known for her precision, her elegance, and her silence.

Arina didn't cry, not even when her father died. She didn't laugh easily. Didn't allow herself to love.

What she did do was build.

Every line she drew. Every wall she raised. Every arch she designed, it was all an attempt to control something she could not name.

Until the migraines began. Unbearable. Vivid.

Each time, she saw flickers of a city on water. A girl in a crimson dress. The scent of salt and hot iron. A scream trapped in stone.

Then, during a site visit to an old Venetian palazzo, she found a coat buried beneath rubble – wool worn thin, lined with unfamiliar stitching. When she touched it, her vision blurred.

And she fell.

1503 / Venice

She awoke to bells. The air brined. The alleyways close.

She was Elisabetta, daughter of a renowned sculptor. A girl whose hands were as skilled as any master's, but whose work was forbidden to be seen. Women were not allowed to chisel beauty from marble. Not allowed to sign their names.

So she created it in secret. By torchlight, beneath her father's studio, she carved angels and grief alike.

Until the day her work was discovered.

Her father claimed it was his. And the doge awarded him a commission that would last generations.

Elisabetta vanished from history. But her ache lived on.

Arina lived as her for weeks, the sorrow of being unseen settling into her bones like dust.

When she returned to her own time, she collapsed at the edge of the Grand Canal clutching a broken chisel she did not bring with her.

She began to weep for the first time in years.

And days later, she redesigned a cathedral entrance she'd been stuck on for months.

This time, she carved a single wing into the stone arch, delicate, defiant. And signed it, in the corner: "E. L."

A tribute to the girl who was never allowed to finish her masterpiece. And who had been remembered at last.

Chapter Eighteen: The Silence Beneath the Floorboards

He didn't speak until he was nearly six.

Even then, Kazuo's words came only in whispers — not of modern things, but of places he had never seen. Temples in fog. Rooms lit by paper lanterns. A garden with stones arranged like a constellation.

His parents said he was sensitive. Teachers called it a delay. But he heard music in wind chimes that others didn't, and sometimes cried when he stepped into certain rooms, as though they remembered him before he knew himself.

At seventeen, during a school trip to a Kyoto heritage site, Kazuo wandered off into a crumbling merchant house. Alone, he knelt to adjust his shoelace and felt a hollow sound beneath the tatami mat.

He pulled it back.

And there – wrapped in silk yellowed with centuries – was the coat.

The moment he touched it, his breath vanished.

1601 / Kyoto

He opened his eyes in a world of quiet grace and danger.

He was Hana, a girl trained as a geisha but burdened with a secret; she was fluent in the language of ink. Not just brushstrokes, but poetry, calligraphy, hidden messages meant for rebellion.

Her brother had died smuggling information to resistance fighters. Now she carried on his cause, in silence, in shadow, through scrolls disguised as love letters and haiku.

But the shogun's men were closing in. The walls had ears. The paper had spies.

Hana's hands were steady, but her heart bled each time she wrote a name that might die.

Kazuo, inside her skin, felt every breath, every brushstroke. The weight of silence. The threat of being seen. The yearning to speak.

And the fear that words – the very thing she loved – could cost her everything.

When the raid came, Hana hid the coat beneath the floor. She did not run. She did not beg.

She looked her captors in the eye and whispered:

"Ink outlives blades."

Kazuo woke in the present, breathless on the floor of the merchant house, still clutching the silk-wrapped coat.

He didn't speak for three days.

Then, in front of his family, he took up a brush and began to write – kanji after kanji, the strokes both ancient and his own. Poems flowed. Paintings followed.

He began teaching children with selective mutism.

Not by speech. But through ink.

On the wall of his studio, he wrote: "Every silence holds a name. Every name holds a thread."

The coat remained sealed in glass nearby, but it shimmered every time he passed, as if the silence between them still spoke.

Chapter Nineteen: The Bones of the Earth

Malik had always walked the desert like it was a question.

A geologist by training, he studied rocks, layers, and fossils. But beneath the science, something deeper pulled at him, something older.

He couldn't explain why he was drawn to places others avoided. Why the wind sometimes felt like breath. Why certain dry riverbeds made his eyes sting with grief.

His colleagues said he was eccentric. A "feeling scientist." But Malik knew he was listening to something they couldn't hear.

For years, the dreams haunted him. Visions of burning fields. Of chains biting into wrists. Of bones buried not in tombs but beneath broken tracks.

Of a name he never spoke aloud: Ayo.

It was during a dig near the Nile – meant to uncover prehistoric fish fossils – when everything changed.

He struck something soft, layered under mud and stone. Not bone. Not fossil.

Cloth.

Wrapped tight around leather. Old. Fragile. Sacred.

It was a coat.

As his fingers brushed its seam, the sky pulsed – just once – and everything went black.

1898 / Sudan

He woke to a scream.

He was barefoot, thin, and sunburned, a boy no older than thirteen. His name came not as memory, but as instinct: Ayo.

He had been taken weeks earlier in a raid. His village burned. His mother – last seen reaching for him as soldiers dragged him into the bush – never reappeared in his dreams. Only her voice. Only her song.

Now he was one of hundreds.

Forced to build a railway under British colonial command. Their purpose was war. Their bodies were fuel.

The labour was relentless. Sleep was a mercy never granted. Water was rationed like gold. Disease tore through the camp, and those who collapsed were left where they fell.

Ayo's job was to break and move stone for the tracks. He bled from his hands daily. Each strike of the pick echoed through his bones like a prayer unanswered.

But the dreams followed him here, too.

Whispers of another life, strange devices, quiet libraries, a coat that hummed like the wind.

And in the silence of night, while others whimpered or wept, Ayo remembered the stories his grandfather once told:

"The earth does not forget its dead. It sings them into the stone. That is why our feet burn when we walk over sorrow."

Ayo began to speak these stories again, in low voice, into the soil as he worked, planting memories where pain had grown.

And Malik, inside him, listened.

One night, during a dust storm, a boy named Sefu tried to escape.

He was caught. They beat him until his breath stopped.

Ayo buried him beneath the railway by moonlight, etching a single stone with the boy's name using only a bent nail.

Sefu – Still Here.

In that moment, Malik wept for the first time in years. Because it wasn't just Ayo's grief anymore.

It was his.

When he returned to the present – flung breathless into the heat of modern Khartoum – Malik didn't speak for three days.

He wandered the streets in silence, barefoot, still feeling the taste of dust on his tongue.

But the dreams had shifted.

Now he saw the faces clearly. Heard names. Remembered stories once lost to empire and time.

He founded a cultural archive – not of statues or bones, but of voices.

He visited villages. Sat with elders. Collected lullabies, grave chants, and the whispered names of those who had vanished without trace.

And in every workshop he taught, he began with these words:

"We suffer today not because we are cursed. We suffer because we are carrying lives that were never allowed to finish their story."

In the corner of his archive, behind glass, the coat hangs still.

And beneath it, on a carved stone, sit five simple words: "The earth remembers for us."

Epilogue: True Threads

These are not imagined tales. They are living echoes, real lives, real people, whose transformations remind us that the past is not gone. It is waiting to be remembered, and once it is, healing begins.

Chapter Twenty: The Enchanted Mirror – A Life Remembered

How The Loveday Method Helped One Woman Reclaim Her Voice

They called her Lena. A quiet woman. Capable, kind, composed. But inside, she was drowning.

She laughed at the right times, worked hard, and cared for others. But behind her eyes lived a silence she could never name. She carried a sadness that didn't seem to belong to her.

Every relationship ended in distance. Every moment of success felt undeserved. She spoke of shame without a source. Grief with no shape.

She would later say, "It was like I was haunted, but the ghost was inside me."

Lena came to her first session reluctantly. "It's not therapy," a friend had said. "It's something different. Something deep."

She expected nothing. She sat politely. She listened.

And then, the moment came.

Her eyes closed. Her breath slowed. And something shifted, the walls of logic softened, and a memory rose.

Not a memory she could explain.

A forest. A small wooden cottage. The smell of lavender and fire smoke.

And a mirror.

Inside the mirror, she saw herself, but not as she was now. Younger. Dressed in heavy skirts. A girl with strong hands and sad eyes. She was scrubbing floors, humming an old folk song. One Lena had never heard, but somehow, knew the words to.

The girl in the mirror had a bruise on her wrist.

And a truth in her throat that had never been spoken.

The session carried her deeper.

She wasn't told the story. She felt it.

She was Margot, a servant in a country estate in 1879. Wrongfully blamed for something she did not do. Silenced. Disgraced. Sent away.

She never told anyone what happened in that house. She died in childbirth, buried in an unmarked grave.

But the echo of her story lived on. In Lena. In the pain that never made sense. In the voice she had spent her whole life suppressing.

When Lena came back from that session, she was shaking. Tears poured out; not of sadness, but of release.

She spoke for two hours straight. Not in fear. In freedom.

"It wasn't me who was ashamed. It was her. And I've been carrying it all my life. I didn't know why I couldn't trust anyone. Why I didn't believe I deserved kindness. But now... I remember. And I forgive us both."

She returned for four more sessions. Each time, a deeper thread unravelled, and her voice grew stronger.

She laughed without apology. She began painting again. She reconnected with her estranged mother – and told her everything. Not the details. The truth.

Today, Lena helps others find their voice. She volunteers at a women's shelter. And every morning, before she leaves the house, she looks in the mirror.

Not to check her reflection. But to remember the girl who once couldn't speak. And the woman who now can.

"The Loveday Method didn't give me a new life," she says. "It helped me remember the one I lost. And called me back to live it fully."

Chapter Twenty One: The Boy Who Carried a Century of Fear

Henry was born with an old name, one that felt borrowed from another era. Even as a child, his mother said he had "ancient eyes."

He never played like the others. He asked questions about death before he knew how to spell the word.

From the age of five, he woke in terror, heart racing, throat tight, dreams full of smoke and steel. His parents called them night terrors. Doctors tried their best.

But the fear never left.

At school, he was bright but distant. At home, he would sit at windows during storms, whispering things he couldn't explain; prayers in a language no one taught him.

By twenty, he'd learned to mask it. But he still carried that feeling:

"I don't belong here."

It was a winter evening in 2046. London was slick with rain. Henry ducked into an old shop for shelter — the kind of place that looked like it had been forgotten by time.

The sign above was so faded it was unreadable. Inside, it smelled of wax, smoke, and something almost like rosemary. The man behind the counter was middle-aged, dressed in a waistcoat and tie; old-fashioned, elegant, and calm.

"You look frozen," he said, eyes twinkling. "Soup?"

Henry nodded, grateful.

As the warmth spread through him, he noticed the shop more closely. It wasn't just old — it was wrong for the time. Lanterns glowed instead of lights. Books with leather spines lined the walls. A single ticking clock hung above a velvet curtain.

Then he saw it — in the far corner: a tiny door. No more than a metre high.

It creaked open, though no one had touched it. Something shimmered behind it. Henry stepped through.

The coat was waiting.

It was impossibly old. Dusty, frayed, yet humming with something alive. The moment he touched it, it wrapped around him – not with fabric, but with recognition.

He didn't fall. He remembered.

1327 / England

A monastery. Stone walls. Candlelight. Cold.

He was Brother Henricus, a monk in his early thirties, quiet, brilliant, and deeply afraid. Not of God. Not of war.

But of truth.

Henricus had once healed with herbs, with words, with compassion. But he had seen too much torture disguised as faith, too much cruelty justified by dogma.

He had witnessed his friend, Brother Theo, taken and burned for what they called heresy. His crime? Speaking Latin words that questioned the Church's control over fear.

And Henricus had said nothing. He had watched. Then turned away.

For years, he buried it in silence. But the guilt became illness. The fear turned to trembling. And the body began to wither.

He died of "madness," they said. But it was memory that killed him.

Henry felt every heartbeat. Every lash of guilt. Every scream that Henricus could not silence.

And in one moment – one aching, final act – he saw himself kneeling by the fire, writing Theo's name into the margins of a sacred book. Hiding it. Preserving it.

"Let one soul remember him."

And Henry, now back in his own body, whispered:

"I remember."

He woke back in the shop. The door was gone. The coat hanging quietly behind glass.

The man at the counter only smiled. "You made it back."

Henry left the shop with his chest open like never before. He felt the same. And entirely different.

The panic attacks lessened. The dreams shifted. He no longer feared death.

Because he now knew he had already lived and carried a fear that was never truly his.

Today, Henry studies medieval history. He translates forgotten texts. And in every margin, he writes a single name: Theo.

"We are the voice for those who were silenced. Their fears live in us, until we choose to free them."

Chapter Twenty Two: The One Who Knew His Name

There are moments when the soul stops walking in one direction. Moments when time folds quietly and the past looks into the eyes of the future. And they both whisper the same name.

It had been weeks since Geoffrey guided Leah through her future life. Weeks since the image of the coat, glowing with remembered lives, refused to leave him.

He could still see her, Amari, walking corridors of light, guiding souls through what she called The Return. And when he looked into Leah's eyes that day, he wasn't just looking at her future.

He was looking at his own.

Not in form, but in meaning.

The Book had changed, too. It pulsed differently now. It no longer revealed only the past, but began offering glimpses of what was unfolding ahead.

Sometimes, Geoffrey would hear whispers during sessions that hadn't yet occurred. See symbols no one had drawn. Feel the presence of someone nearby, just beyond the veil.

Someone familiar. Someone... watching.

It was raining when the young man arrived.

He was no more than twenty-one. His coat was soaked. His accent was unfamiliar. But he carried something ancient in his eyes, and something impossible in his words.

He didn't knock. He just waited, quietly, outside Geoffrey's door, as though he had been expected.

Geoffrey opened it. And the man smiled.

"It's good to see you again, Alarion."

Geoffrey froze.

Only two people had ever called him that name. Both had been in trance. Both had been in lifetimes hundreds, sometimes thousands of years apart.

"Who are you?" he asked quietly.

The young man stepped inside, looking around the room. His eyes softened as they landed on the Book.

"My name is Cassian," he said. "I came through your teachings, but not from here. Not from this time."

He placed a small device – round, smooth, humming lightly – on the table.

"You wrote about it," he said. "In the Archive. In the Library of Light. I followed your work for years before I found you."

Geoffrey's mouth went dry. "But I haven't written that yet."

Cassian only smiled. "Not yet. But you will. Because I read it."

He wasn't from the past. He wasn't from now. He was a seeker from the future, one shaped by Geoffrey's legacy, who had returned to awaken the final truth; that the healer was not just remembering past lives, he was living in the beginning of something that would change the way souls moved through time itself.

That night, Geoffrey sat in silence.

The rain fell. The Book glowed faintly. And he realised he had become the echo.

The echo someone else would follow. The one whose story would ripple forward. Whose words would be remembered before they were ever written.

And in that silence, the Book finally turned its last page. Not to close the story, but to begin a new one.

Some echoes reach backward. Some spiral forward. But the rarest of all are the ones that meet themselves, and remember who they came here to be.

Chapter Twenty Three: The Keeper's Return

Some seekers are not born in the past. They are born in the echoes of the legacy you haven't written yet, drawn to the moment where it all began.

Cassian stood quietly in Geoffrey's study, his fingers lightly brushing the surface of the old desk. To him, this space was sacred. A myth, made real.

Geoffrey watched him, curious, unsure. The presence of this young man didn't feel like a disruption. It felt like a key. One that had been missing all along.

"You said you came through my teachings," Geoffrey finally asked. "From where? When?"

Cassian turned to him and smiled, his voice calm, his presence steady.

"I was born in 2139. The world is different now, fractured, but healing. We've come to understand that time isn't what we thought it was. And that healing doesn't move in one direction."

He stepped closer to the Book. Not the glowing, living version Geoffrey had seen in trance, but the worn, leather-bound one in his hands.

Cassian reached into his coat pocket and pulled out a small, crystalline object, shimmering faintly with light that didn't belong to this century.

"This is why I'm here." Cassian placed the crystal on the table. Immediately, the Book pulsed. The air thickened. Time slowed.

And then, something impossible happened: a new page appeared, one Geoffrey had never seen, one he hadn't written. On it was a title: "The Spectacles of Memory: The Guardian's Passage"

Geoffrey reached toward it, but his hand shook. "That chapter. It's from the future."

Cassian nodded. "You wrote it fifty years from now. It was sealed with intention, meant only to be opened at the moment you would understand it. That moment is now."

Cassian explained that The Loveday Method, as powerful as it already was, was never meant to be the end. It was the activation point, a way to remember the past, so the future could be shaped deliberately.

Not just to heal what had been, but to consciously plant what could be.

"The Method created a generation of returners," Cassian said. "People who learned to walk time like memory, to change timelines through healing, to prevent suffering before it could take root."

"But none of it could exist without you. Without this moment. Without your return to yourself."

He paused. "You weren't just meant to remember the past, Geoffrey. You were meant to teach us how to remember the future."

"But why now?" Geoffrey asked. "Why are you here? Why this moment?"

Cassian's expression turned solemn.

"Because there's a fracture forming. Something old is waking again, something that was never healed properly. It's echoing forward, pulling apart everything we've built. You are the only one who can reach that memory. Because it's yours. But you buried it lifetimes ago. We need you to go back one final time and bring forward the truth that was never spoken. The one that created the first silence."

Geoffrey felt the weight of the words. Not fear. Not pressure. Just a strange kind of gravity. Like a star collapsing inward. A soul returning home.

He looked at the crystal. Then at the Book. Then at the young man who knew his name before he ever spoke it.

"What happens if I find it?" Geoffrey asked.

Cassian smiled. "Then the world remembers. And time begins to heal itself."

Chapter Twenty Four: The First Silence

Before the Book was written, before the Method had a name, before any seeker walked the bridge between lives, there was one soul, one vow, and one forgotten wound that set it all in motion.

Geoffrey had guided hundreds, perhaps thousands, through time. But this was different.

This wasn't a soul memory rising to meet him. This wasn't someone else's pain calling for release.

This was a summons. One he had delayed for lifetimes. One that only now, with Cassian watching, the Book open and the crystal humming at his side, he could finally answer.

He sat down. Breathed in. Closed his eyes. And whispered to the soul: "Take me back. Back to the first wound. Back to where the silence began."

There was no staircase this time. No gentle descent. No guiding voice.

There was only light. Blinding. Soft. And full of knowing.

When the light faded, Geoffrey stood barefoot on cracked white stone. Beneath him: an endless desert. Above: stars that shimmered like they were watching him.

In his hands: a pen made of fire. And around his neck, the spectacles.

He was not Geoffrey. He was not Alarion. Not yet. His name was Kael. And he was the first.

Kael belonged to an ancient civilisation long since erased from the surface of the earth, a culture that lived not by law, but by resonance. By soul-encoded memory.

They were scribes of truth. They didn't write history. They remembered it, before it happened.

And Kael was the youngest scribe ever chosen. Not because he had knowledge, but because he could hear the soul of time.

Every word he wrote carried power. Every truth he spoke shaped reality. But then he made one choice.

One terrible, human, loving choice. He kept something secret.

A truth he was meant to share. A message from the future. A glimpse of destruction.

But to speak it would have meant exile. So he held it. Buried it.

And that silence, that single withheld truth, was the first fracture.

The one that echoed down lifetimes.

Geoffrey, remembering as Kael, fell to his knees in the memory. The fire-pen slipped from his hand.

"I was afraid," he whispered. "I didn't want to lose them. So I stayed quiet. And the world changed."

Cassian's voice reached through the trance. "What was the truth, Kael?"

"That the timekeepers had lied. That the cycle of peace was ending. That we needed to awaken the others."

"But I said nothing. I choose comfort over calling. And I watched it all fall."

It was in the ashes of that fall, after the temples had crumbled, after the great knowledge had been scattered, that Kael made a vow:

"In every life that follows, I will guide others to remember. I will build the bridge I once refused to walk. And I will never silence the soul again."

That vow became a current. A pulse through every incarnation. Through Alarion. Through Geoffrey. Through every seeker who had walked into the Book.

And with it, The Loveday Method was born. Not in practice, but in purpose.

Geoffrey gasped as he emerged from trance. His hands trembled. Tears streamed silently down his face.

Cassian was waiting. Not with questions, but with stillness.

Geoffrey didn't speak for a long time. When he did, his voice was raw.

"I remember now. The silence wasn't theirs. It was mine. And I've been breaking it ever since."

The Book shimmered. A final page appeared, blank. Geoffrey reached for the crystal pen Cassian had brought from the future. It fit in his hand like it had been waiting all this time.

He wrote: "The soul remembers what the mind forgets. And when truth is finally spoken, time begins to heal.

This was the beginning. And this is the return. The Book is open. The silence has ended.

Chapter Twenty Five: The Echo in Your Hands

Some books don't just tell stories. They remember you.

So here we are, at the final page. Not an ending. A beginning.

You've walked through memory. You've seen lives unfold that were not yours, but somehow, you felt them anyway.

Perhaps that's because they were yours. Or echoes of them. Fragments left in your bones, in your dreams, in your breath.

This is more than a book. It always has been.

It is a remembering.

The Book of Echoes

Some say it's a myth. A book not written in ink, but woven into the fabric of time itself.

But you've held it. Page by page. Memory by memory.

The Book of Echoes is real, not because it exists in the world, but because it stirs in your soul.

Every time you breathe more freely, cry without knowing why, or feel seen by a story that shouldn't know you, the Book is open.

The Enchanted Spectacles

And what of the Spectacles? The ones whispered of in dreams, the lenses through which truth is finally clear?

They are not worn on the face. They are worn by the soul. They allow you to see the world not as it is, but as it truly has been. As it still could be.

You may already be wearing them. You wouldn't know it. Not at first.

But when the unseen becomes familiar, when the impossible feels intimate, you'll know.

The Coat of a Thousand Lives

And the coat? The one that appeared without warning, carried across lifetimes, worn by the brave and the broken and the ones who dared to remember?

That coat is no ordinary garment. It is a mark of remembrance. A soul-cloak. A quiet symbol that you are part of something much older and much more powerful than your current name.

You may not see it yet. But you've felt it. The shiver. The knowing. The sense that something ancient is draped across your shoulders, even when you walk alone.

That coat chooses those ready to walk between lifetimes. To heal. To remember. To lead others back.

If you've heard it calling, you're not imagining it. You're being called.

When The Loveday Method came to me, I thought I was the teacher. But I was the student. The translator. The keeper of a vow made long before this lifetime began.

Now, I pass this to you.

Not as knowledge, but as a thread. You are part of this story now. In fact, you always were.

I'm not asking you to believe. Only to remember.

And to wonder: What if this feeling in your chest is not fear, but memory? What if the grief that never made sense is inherited? What if the longing you carry isn't for a place, but for a time you've already lived?

You are not broken. You are not late. You are not alone.

You are remembering.

And your remembering will help others do the same.

So I'll leave you with this: You are the echo. You are the bridge. You are the next author of the Book.

When you're ready, close these pages.

But know this; the Book of Echoes, the Enchanted Spectacles, and the Coat of a Thousand Lives will never close on you.

Not now. Not ever.

Final Reflection

"The Thread Has Always Known Your Name"

You have walked through echoes. You have worn the Coat. Peered through the Spectacles. Opened the Book. And somewhere along the way, you may have felt it; a shiver, a stillness, a recognition.

Not just of the stories. But of yourself.

Because this journey was never only about the past. It was never only about other people's pain. It was about the part of you that has been waiting to awaken.

The part that remembers.

The grief that didn't start in this life. The fear you were told was "just anxiety." The dream that made no sense, until now.

The Loveday Method, at its heart, is not a technique.

It is a remembering.

It is the moment you step through the veil and realise the answers were never lost, only sleeping in the deeper chambers of your soul.

It is the bridge between lifetimes. Between the breath of the body and the memory of the eternal.

And now, you stand at that bridge. Not to look back, but to walk forward, knowing more of who you truly are.

So what now?

Perhaps you follow the thread. Perhaps you sit in stillness and listen for the voice beneath your thoughts. Perhaps you guide others, just as you have been guided.

Because the world is full of those still carrying stories that were never theirs. Still searching for a reason behind the ache they can't explain.

And now you know: It's not madness. It's memory. And memory can be healed. Not through forgetting, but through the sacred act of remembering and returning it to time.

So, whether this book was your beginning or only a return to something you've always known, may you walk forward with open eyes? May you listen to what speaks without words? May you trust the ache is not the end, but the invitation?

And above all, may you know this: You were never lost. You were only waiting for the thread to call you home.

— Geoffrey Loveday

Dedication

To those who carry silent stories; may you one day find the words to speak them.

To the ones haunted by dreams not their own, you are not broken. You are remembering.

And to the forgotten: You were never truly lost.

This is for you.

Coming In 2025

The Crystal: A Touch Through Time

Fourth in the Series of Seven Books

The Origin of The Loveday Method®

A Heptalogy

By

Geoffrey Loveday

www.ingramcontent.com/pod-product-compliance
Lightning Source LLC
Chambersburg PA
CBHW050612100526
44584CB00038B/2931